THE MASS
for Children

The reprinting of this book is dedicated in loving
memory of the members of the Kriley family.

Oh Mary, conceived without sin,
pray for us who have recourse to thee.

Cover and book design by Ted Schluenderfritz

Images on pages 44, 51 and 54 © Holy Family Catholic Church CC
BY-SA 3.0 Nheyob. All other images are in the public domain

Laudamus Press
P. O. Box 251
Hamlin, Pa 18427
www.laudamus-te.com

THE MASS
for Children

BY REV WILLIAM R. KELLY, M.A.

Laudamus press

AT THE
BEGINNING OF MASS

ONE DAY a boy was asked to make the sign of the cross. Being a little fellow he did not know what was meant. But when someone said: "Bless yourself, my boy," he knew just what to do; and raising his right hand to his forehead, he began to say: "In the name of the Father, and of the Son, and of the Holy Ghost. Amen."

The priest begins Mass with these holy words, and so do we. When we make the sign of the cross, it is like a signal to God. It tells God we are beginning Mass in His name and for His sake.

Surely we want to start Mass well, don't we? Then let us go to church early so that we can make the sign of the cross when the priest does.

I CONFESS

At the "Confiteor" A FEW MOMENTS after the priest has made the sign of the cross, he bends over and says a prayer which we all know well. He says: "I confess to Almighty God," and we say it with him. The priest bows his head, and so do we—because we are sorry for our sins and are ashamed of them.

We strike our breast three times. It is, indeed, through our own fault that we have sinned. No one else can be blamed.

THE PRIEST KISSES THE ALTAR.

WHEN THE PRIEST walks up the steps, we think of Our Lord and how He walked up Mount Calvary with His cross. The cross on the priest's back reminds us that he is taking the place of Jesus.

Next, the priest kisses the altar. If we were to lift up the cloth in the middle of the altar, we would see a small square stone. It is this stone which he kisses. Inside the stone is a little hollow space, and in this space are small pieces of bone from the bodies of certain saints.

These saints died for Our Lord. Some of them were only young children. Pagan people who did not believe in God, burned them to death or let them be eaten by wild beasts, but they could not make them leave the true religion.

The priest now goes to the big book which we call the Missal. He reads a part of a holy song written by a man named David. David was a shepherd who became a king. He was a brave soldier, too. Best of all, he was a saint, and one of God's leaders.

LORD, HAVE MERCY

At the "Kyrie Eleison"

AFTER HE READS a while, the priest moves to the middle of the altar. If we listen we shall hear first his voice, and then the voice of the altar boys. They are saying the prayer: "Lord have mercy on us." "Christ have mercy on us."

This is a wonderful prayer. When sick people said it, Our Lord made them well again. It was as though they said: "Be kind to us, pity us; do not let us suffer." That is what mercy means. If we ask God to have mercy on us, He will help us, too.

4

GLORY BE TO GOD

LOOK AT THE PICTURE of the priest. He is saying: "Glory be to God on high, and on earth peace to men of good will." Every Catholic child knows these words from the story of Christmas. Angels sang them on the night Jesus was born.

At the "Gloria"

In this prayer "Glory to God," the priest says many beautiful things. Here are some of his words: "We praise Thee; we bless Thee, we glorify Thee, we give Thee thanks."

Then he says, "O Lord God, Lamb of God who takest away the sins of the world, have mercy on us."

The lamb reminds us of the Jewish religion before Our Lord came. The Jews used to take the best lamb they could get and bring it to the priest, that he might offer its life to God. As the lamb's life was taken away, the people prayed that their sins might be taken away forever. The lamb was punished instead of the people.

Gerard David,
Nativity, 1495

When a lamb was killed, and

offered to God by a priest, that was called a "sacrifice." Our Lord is called the Lamb of God because He offered up His life for the sins of all people. He was punished instead of us. His death on the cross was a sacrifice. We call it the, "sacrifice of the Cross."

detail of *Sacrifice of the Old Covenant* by Peter Paul Ruben

THE LORD BE WITH YOU

IN THIS PICTURE we see the priest turning to the people.

At the "Dominus vobiscum"

"The Lord be with you,"
he says.

The altar boy answers for the people. They say: "And with your spirit." The priest prays that God will stay with us, now and always. And we pray that God will stay with our priest. This is what we mean when we say: "And with your spirit."

If Our Lord is with us, we are sure to be happy. He is with us as long as we keep from mortal sin. He will not stay with people who have mortal sins on their souls.

When we see the priest turning around to us at Mass, we pray for him. We say: "Oh God stay always in the priest's soul; and help him, now, to offer Mass well." Good people always pray for the priest.

The priest turns to us and says: "The Lord be with you," he holds up his hands. Then he goes to the book to read a prayer for us. While he is praying there, he still holds his hands up.

That makes us think of a story. It is about a

Nicolas Poussin
1593/94 – 1665
Joshua Fights Amalek

man who won a battle by holding up his hands in prayer.

Once upon a time the pagans marched out to fight God's people. When Moses, the Prophet of God, saw them coming he sent soldiers to stop them.

Moses went to the top of a hill to watch the fight. He rose up his hands, and prayed God to help His people to win. As long as Moses held his hands in prayer, God's people kept on winning. But when he got tired and dropped his hands, they began to lose.

So two men helped Moses to hold up his hands, and he prayed and prayed, until at last the pagans were beaten and driven away.

The priest is like Moses. He is praying for us that we may win the fight against our enemy, the devil.

THE EPISTLE

Do you see where the priest is standing now? We call this side of the altar the Epistle side because it is here that the Epistle is read. The Epistles are holy letters.

At the Epistle

Most of them were written by St. Paul. The people were glad to get St. Paul's letters. They kept them like a treasure.

They read them out loud in the church Sunday after Sunday. They also read letters written by St. Peter and St. John, and other apostles of Jesus.

It was God who helped the apostles to write these letters, or Epistles.

The Epistles are the sacred word of God.

THE BOOK IS MOVED

THE BOY NOW TAKES the book from the Epistle Side and carries it to the Gospel side of the altar. This changing of the book is to remind us of the change from the Jewish to the Catholic religion.

The Jewish religion was meant to get people ready for Our Lord. When He came, He gave us our perfect religion.

The Jews were waiting a long time for Our Lord to come. How sad it was that when He did come, many of them would not believe in Him.

In this picture we see Jesus weeping as He looks at Jerusalem, the City of the Jews. The Jews were his own people. He came to save them; yet they turned their backs on Him and went away.

As the book is moved, we shall pray God never to let us go away from Him by sin.

Enrique Simonet
(1866–1927)
He wept over it

THE GOSPEL

At the Gospel

THIS PICTURE shows the priest reading the Gospel. The place where he is standing is called Gospel side of the altar. In the Holy Gospel are the very words of Our Lord. There, too, we find the story of the wonderful things He did while He was on earth.

The people stand up when the altar boy moves the books to the Gospel side. They stand to show Our Lord that they honor and respect His Gospel, and are ready to do what He tells them. To stand is a sign of honor and respect. We stand when the teacher comes into the room. We stand for the song of our country. A soldier stands when the flag goes by.

How proud we are to stand up for the Gospel of Jesus! We are soldiers of Our Lord. To Him we say: "Here I am, O Lord! I am ready to do whatever You want!"

What is it that God wants us to do? He wants us to know Him, to love Him, to serve Him in this life and to be happy with Him in heaven.

As the priest begins the Gospel, he makes a little cross on his forehead, lips, and heart—and so do we. One cross we make on our forehead, asking God to help our minds, that we may understand the Gospel. The next cross we make on our lips, that we may speak like Catholics who believe in the Gospel. The last cross we make on our hearts, that they may be filled with love for the Gospel of Our Lord.

The apostles had great love for Our Lord. He was always in their minds and hearts. They went to far-off places to speak to the pagans about Him.

Even to this day good missionaries are going all over the world to teach the pagans about Our Lord and His religion. Good Catholics are glad to help these missionaries.

I BELIEVE IN GOD

AFTER THE GOSPEL has been read, the priest goes to the mid- *At the "Credo"* dle of the altar. There he says the prayer: "I believe in God." When he kneels, we kneel too in honor of Infant Jesus.

How happy we are to be Catholics! We believe in God and in all He teaches us. Let us tell Him so:

Oh my God, I believe in You;
What you say is always true;
I believe what the Church says too,
Because its words have come from You.

Whenever Our Lord met people who really believed in Him, He was always glad to help them.

One day two blind men followed Him, crying out and saying: "Jesus have mercy on us." And Jesus said to them "Do you believe that I can do this to you?" They said to him, "Yes, Lord." They knew Jesus could make them see if He wanted to. They showed that they did believe in Him. So Our Lord opened their eyes, and at last they were able to see.

Because the blind men believed in Our Lord, He heard their prayer and gave them what they asked. Jesus did many other things for those who showed that they believed in Him. If we believe in God, we will love Him and we will do everything He wants us to do. Bad boys and girls may try to get us away from God they may ask us to stay away from Mass. But let us be like St. Agnes and say: "No, never will I leave God."

Vicente Masip
Martyrdom of
St Agnes

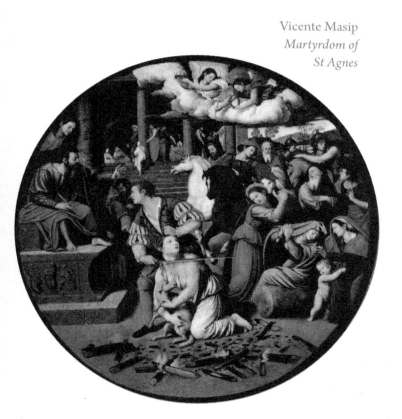

"We'll punish you in terrible way, and then we'll kill you," they said to her, "unless you do as we tell you." Did she? No, she let them kill her, but they couldn't touch her holy soul, which went right to heaven.

Brave little St. Agnes! How proud we are of her, and of the many other children who died for Our Lord because they believed in Him and loved Him.

THE PRIEST OFFERS THE BREAD AND WINE

At the Offertory THE TIME has now come for the priest to take the veil off the gold cup. The gold cup is called the "chalice." From the top of the chalice, he takes a little gold plate on which the round white bread has been resting.

In this picture we see him holding up the plate, with both hands, as he offers the bread to God. First, he offers it for himself, then for

the people who are present in the Church and
then for all good Christians both living and
dead. Next he takes the chalice to the side
of the altar, where the altar boys are ready
to give wine and water. When the wine and

water are mixed, they can never be separated. This reminds us to pray that we may never be separated from Jesus.

Now the priest holds up the chalice, offering it to Our Lord. He begs Our Lord that this chalice may save us and save the whole world. When the priest offers the bread and wine, we think of Our Lord as He lay on the cross offering Himself to the Father. He offered Himself to be a sacrifice for the sins of

Gerard David
*Christ Nailed to
the Cross*, c. 1481

all people. The Jewish people offered lambs to be a sacrifice for sin. But Our Lord offered himself. He is the Lamb of God who takes away the sins of the whole world.

THE PRIEST WASHES HIS HANDS

THE ALTAR BOYS are waiting now at the side of the altar. They have a towel, a basin and a pitcher of water for the priest to wash his hands.

At the "Lavabo"

While they are waiting, the priest raises his eyes to heaven. He asks the Holy Ghost to come and bless the sacrifice which he is going to offer to Almighty God. Then he washes his hands. This is a sign telling us how clean our souls must be in God's sight.

Let us pray that God will wash us more and more, so that there will not be even a tiny sin on our souls.

HOLY, HOLY, HOLY

At the "Sanctus" WE ARE GETTING NEARER and nearer to the wonderful moment of the Mass. We say to ourselves: "Our Lord is coming; Our Lord in coming." He is coming to be our sacrifice.

Now the priest prays aloud. He is thanking God, the Father, the Son and the Holy

26

Ghost. He is praising God; and all the angels in heaven are praising God with him.

His prayer is like a holy song with a fine chorus. When the altar boy rings the bell, we join in the chorus of that holy song, and say with the priest and the angels:

"Holy, Holy, Holy Lord, God of Hosts, Heaven and earth are full of Thy Glory."

Now we add more words of praise and welcome to Jesus. We say:

"Hosanna in the highest.
Blessed is He that comes in the
name of the Lord.
Hosanna in the highest."

In the time of Our Lord these words were shouted by a great crowd. They had just heard about Our Lord raising a dead man to life. How proud they were of Jesus! They had a procession for Him when He came to their

city. Men and women and children waved branches and shouted a welcome to Jesus.

Entry Into Jerusalem, Pedro Orrente, c1620

Our Lord was their hero. They spread their coats on the street to make a carpet for Him. Everybody cheered and cried out: "Hosanna! Hosanna!" That was their way of saying, "Hurrah! Hurrah!"

Let us think of all this when the bell rings. It rings to tell us that Jesus is coming. It is now our turn to welcome Him.

At the first sound of the bell everybody kneels. There is silence in the church. Even the voice of the priest is hushed. Let us watch and pray.

The bells ring again—just one little ring— as the priest hold his hands over the bread and wine. He holds his hands out flat, with the palms down, as we see in the picture (on the next page).

Jewish priests, of long ago, used to stretch their hands like this over the lambs they were to sacrifice. When they did so, the people knew it was a sign that their sins were being put upon the lamb.

When our priest holds his hands over the bread and wine, let us remember again the Jesus is the Lamb of God, who takes away the sins of the world. He is our sacrifice. He

offered Himself to His heavenly Father, and died to take away our sins.

The night before He died, He had His Last Supper with the apostles. Then it was that He changed the bread into His Body and changed the wine into His Blood.

Then it was that He made His apostles priests and gave them power to what He had just done. He gave them power to change bread and wine into His Body and Blood. "As often as you shall do these things," Our Lord said to them, "you shall do them in memory of me." The apostles were taught that whenever they changed the bread and wine, they should show forth the death of the Lord.

The priest is now bending low. He takes the round white bread into his hands.

Philippe de Champaigne (1602–1674) *Last supper*

He looks for a second at the cross over the altar. Then he says the very words that Our Lord said at the Last Supper. He says:

"THIS IS MY BODY."

At the Consecration of the Host

A T ONCE Our Lord comes on the altar. The priest kneels and adores Him. The people bow their heads

THE PRIEST HOLDS UP THE SACRED HOST

At the Elevation of the Host

T HE PRIEST holds up the sacred Host. He wants us to see Jesus. So we raise our eyes and look at Jesus Our Savior. With loving hearts we say to Him: "My Lord and my God." It is the most holy Body of Our Lord.

It is the same good Lord who was at the Last Supper with His apostles. Oh, what

wonderful power God has given to His priests! By their holy words they bring Our Lord down on the altar. By their holy words they bring first His Body, and then His blood. We see Our Lord as though His Blood were separated and apart from His Body. We see Him as though He were a lamb slain for our

sins. Thus do priests show forth the death of the Lord.

When the priest says the words which change the bread into the Body of Our Lord, the altar boy rings the bell three times. It will be rung again when the priest changes the wine into Our Lord's Precious Blood.

While we wait for the bell to ring, let us think of Our Lord suffering on the cross.

Let us think, too, of Our Blessed Lady, as she stood there weeping. She knew why Our Lord was called the "lamb of God." She knew He was going to shed His Blood on the cross, and so be sacrificed like a lamb, to take away our sins. May she help us to understand that here in the Mass the priest shows forth the death of the Lord.

Now we see the priest again bending low. This time the takes in his hands the chalice of wine. He says the words:

Gerard David (circa 1450/1460–1523), Crucifixion, circa 1475

35

"THIS IS MY BLOOD."

THEY ARE THE VERY WORDS Our Lord said over the wine at the Last Supper. At once the wine is changed into Our Lord's Blood. The bell is rung and we bow our heads.

THE PRIEST HOLDS UP THE CHALICE.

AS THE PRIEST holds up the chalice with the Precious Blood of Jesus, we raise our eyes to the altar. With all our hearts we say to Our Lord: "My Jesus, mercy." The Body and the Blood of Our Lord are on the altar. It is the very Body of Jesus which hung on the cross. It is the very Blood of Jesus which was shed for us sinners.

We adore Jesus, for He is our God. We thank him because He died to save our souls.

We tell Him we are sorry for all the sins of our life. We ask Him for everything we need for our souls and bodies.

All is silent again after the bread and wine have changed into the Body and Blood of

Our Lord. But soon, we shall hear the priest
saying a few words out loud. They are words

in which the priest is reminded that even he can fall into sin. That is why he strikes his breast at this time.

Our Lord once told a story about two men who went to church to pray. One man was bold and proud. He thought he was somebody. He even dared to thank God he was not sinful like other men.

At the back of the church, near the door, was the other man, all bent over with shame. He beat his breast because he knew he was a sinner, and he begged God to have mercy on him. God helped that man because he prayed so well; but He would not help the bold, proud man.

When the priest strikes his breast, he remembers Our Lord's story, and so should we.

James Tissot,
(1836-1902)
*The Pharisee
and the Publican*

Let us pray that we shall never become bold or proud. We want God to help us, and so we beg Him to have mercy on us.

39

THE "OUR FATHER"

THE PRIEST IS NOW saying the "Our Father." It is the first *At the "Pater Noster"* long prayer he says aloud after the changing of the bread and wine. It is the best and the most beautiful of all prayers. From it we learn that God is our Father, that we are His children, and that heaven is our home.

40

Our Lord Himself made the "Our Father" and taught it to the apostles. And because the words of this prayer have come from Jesus, we try to say it very well indeed. The apostles said the "Our Father"

Carl Heinrich Bloch (1834–1890), *The Sermon On the Mount*

together with Our Lord. Let us say it together with Him as He looks at us from the altar.

WHEN THE HOST IS BROKEN

A T THE LAST SUPPER Our Lord broke the bread which He had changed into His Body. That is why the priest now breaks the Sacred Host. As we hear the sound of the breaking, let us think with sorrow of our poor Lord. His body was broken by the cruel nails and His Blood was shed for us, that we might be saved from our sins.

LAMB OF GOD

A MOMENT AFTER the breaking of the Host, the priest strikes his breast three times. In a loud voice he says: "Lamb of God, who takest away the sins of the world, have mercy on us." Jesus is the Lamb of God. It was St. John the Baptist who first called Him by this name.

At the
"Agnus Dei"

One morning St. John was talking to some people when Our Lord happened to walk by. As soon as John saw Jesus, he began to cry out: "Behold the Lamb of God."

Two friends of St. John ran after Our Lord to speak to Him. He invited them to come with Him. They became his first apostles. One was St. Andrew and the other was St. John the Apostle.

It was not until after Our Lord had died that they really understood why He was called "The Lamb of God." Then they knew that He was offered up like a lamb. And we know that in the Mass the same lamb is offered too. That is why the priest asks Jesus, the Lamb of God, to have mercy on us.

THE PRIEST RECEIVES
COMMUNION

O LORD, I am not worthy that You should come under my roof; but say the only the word and my soul shall be healed." These are the words that the priest

At the "Domine non sum dignus"

says before he receives Holy Communion. He feels unworthy to receive Our Lord.

Even the apostles felt unworthy to receive Holy Communion. No one, not even an angel, is really fit to receive the Most High God. It is only because God wants us to come that we dare to receive Holy Communion. Three times the priest tells God he is not worthy; and each time he strikes

Paolo Veronese (1528–1588) *El Veronés, Jesús y el centurión*, c. 1571

46

his breast. Then it is that the altar boy rings the bell, so that the people may come up to receive Holy Communion.

The words, "O Lord, I am not worthy" were first spoken by a soldier who came to ask Our Lord to cure his dying servant. Jesus was about to go and do so, when the soldier said: "Lord, I am not worthy that You should come under my roof."

He thought it was not right for him, a sinful man, to bring Jesus into his house. He asked Our Lord to say just one word, and the servant would be cured. Our Lord did what he asked. He cured the servant at that moment. The soldier got his wish because he believed in Our Lord.

No wonder the Church wants the priests to say the words of this soldier before he receives the Body and Blood of Jesus! It is a most beautiful way for him to show his love and respect for Our Lord.

THE PEOPLE RECEIVE
COMMUNION

At the "Ecce, Agnus Dei"

AFTER THE PRIEST has received the Body and Blood of Our Lord, he gives Holy Communion to the people. Here in this picture we see him holding the Sacred Host. "Behold the Lamb of God," he says.

And we know it is Jesus whom he is holding.

We think of our Blessed Lady holding Jesus in her arms. We ask her to help us at this moment. We say to her: "Mother dear, pray for me." And she will.

Marianne Stokes
(1855–1927)
Madonna and Child

Before the priest goes down to the altar rail, he says again, "O Lord, I am not worthy." We say it, too—and mean it. Then, at last, the priest puts Holy Communion on our tongues. It is Jesus, our God.

Now we can adore him, and thank Him for all that He has done for us. We can tell Him how sorry we are for every sin. And we can ask Him for all that we need.

We ask Him to hear our prayer as He heard the prayer of Moses. And He will help us to win the fight against our enemy the devil.

We beg Him to make us love Him as the apostles did, so that we may always keep Him in our minds and hearts.

We pray that we shall be brave like St. Agnes and the other holy children, so that no one may ever be able to make us do what is wrong.

Not like the bold, proud man do we pray; we pray like the poor sinner. We beg God to have mercy on us. We know He will forgive us if we love Him and are really sorry for our sins.

And with all the angels, we shall sing in our hearts to the Lamb of God saying:

> "We praise Thee,
> We bless Thee,
> We glorify Thee;
> We give thanks,
> O Lord God Lamb of God, who takest away the sins of the world."

THE BLESSING

AND NOW THE PRIEST turns to us. He raises his right hand to give us God's blessing. We get down on our knees and make the sign of the cross as the priest says:

> May Almighy God bless you—The Father, the Son, and the Holy Ghost."

52

Our Lord gives us His blessing at the end of Mass just as He gave His blessing to little children long, long ago. How happy we are to get this blessing!

Carl Heinrich Bloch,
Christ with Children

53

THE LAST GOSPEL

RIGHT AFTER the blessing, the priest goes to the Gospel side of the Altar. There he reads *At the Last Gospel* the Gospel of St. John. All the people in the Church stand up, just as they did for the first reading of the Gospel.

We stand proudly, like soldiers of Jesus Christ. We make the sign of His cross on our foreheads and lips and hearts.

At the end of the Gospel, we bend our right knee to the floor and rise again in honor of Our Lord becoming man. Last of all we say what we should never forget to say:

"Thanks be to God."

AN ACT OF
SPIRITUAL COMMUNION

MY JESUS, I believe that You are present in the Most Holy Sacrament.

I love You above all things, and I desire to receive You into my soul.

Since I cannot at this moment receive You sacramentally, come at least spiritually into my heart. I embrace You as if You were already there and unite myself wholly to You. Never permit me to be separated from You. Amen.

CPSIA information can be obtained
at www.ICGtesting.com
Printed in the USA
BVOW11s1133230218
508726BV00006B/34/P